C.O.W.
on a mission

Building a missional business and changing the world!

Benjamin Drury

@Cogiva | fb.com/cogiva | cogiva.com

Published by Cogiva Ltd.
8 Oxford Street, Whitley Bay. NE26 1AE.
www.cogiva.com

Publisher's Cataloguing-in-Publication data
Drury, Benjamin
    COW on a Mission: Building a missional business and changing the world! / Benjamin Drury
        p. cm.
ISBN-10: 1491052287
ISBN-13: 978-1491052280

DEDICATION

To Shelley.
It's finally here.
It's now time for an adventure!

CONTENTS

ACKNOWLEDGMENTS

The last ten years: you've taught me so much; mostly stuff I didn't want to learn at the time, but you're persistent!

My family: you have given so much to make this book happen. It's been a long slog and you've encouraged me all the way. Thank you for your patience, your smiles, your forgiveness, your hugs and your laughter. I love you. (Isabel, Oliver and Henry your names are now officially in print!)

Hannah: your help in turning my rambling thoughts into grammatically correct flowing prose was much needed! Thank you.

Dominic: It takes faith to risk writing a forward for an unproven first time author. Thank you for your grace.

Jesus: you gave us life in all its fullness and a calling to match. This is what you've called me to. Thank you.

FORWARD

In *Cow on a Mission*, Ben's passion for business to be a force for good in the world; and for Christians to be at the forefront of this; and his many qualities including his accessibility, his positivity and his entrepreneurial drive shine through.

If you're thinking of starting a business, already running a business, or just interested in how your work can be more meaningful, *Cow on a Mission* is for you.

It is full of useful insight from Ben and also from those he has learned from on his own journey: ranging from entrepreneurs including Richard Branson and Jack Welch to thought leaders such as Daniel Pink and Patrick Lencioni.

Not only will this book help you think clearly about how to do business and how it can be connected to your mission; it is, like Ben, highly encouraging.

Dominic Llewellyn
September 2013

1 WHAT'S A COW

> *"Business has to give people enriching, rewarding lives or it's simply not worth doing"*
>
> *Richard Branson[1]*

Over the last few years business has had a bit of a bad rap. We're in the middle of a worldwide recession which, for the average household in the UK, shows little sign of improving. People are struggling to pay their bills, sometimes even being forced to choose between paying rent or buying food. Yet at the same time, stories of greed and excess abound.

Businesses are regularly projected in the media as corrupt, greedy and focused on growth at the expense of the underdog. Philanthropy and benevolence have seemingly been consigned to history and rare phenomenon. It is difficult to believe that business can be both a financial success and founded on values of grace, altruism and integrity. Greed is a fundamental canker within the sector which has been allowed to grow unchecked.

There's the story of Bernie Madoff. The former non-executive Chairman of the NASDAQ stock market confessed to be the operator of a Ponzi scheme which is considered to be the largest financial fraud in U.S. history[2] amounting to almost $65 billion. On December 10, 2008, Madoff's sons told authorities how their father had confessed to be involved in "one big lie"[3] as the asset management unit of his firm was a massive Ponzi scheme. He was arrested the next day. Madoff was sentence on June 29, 2009, to the maximum stay of 150 years in federal prison, for conning thousands of Americans out of their hard earned savings.

Take Fred Goodwin's story of greed and abundance which resulted in economic disaster on a national scale. Goodwin's strategy of rapid, aggressive expansion of Royal Bank of Scotland (RBS) to become the world's largest company (with assets of £1.9 trillion[4]) eventually led to the bank being forced to nationalise in 2008 after making the biggest losses in British corporate history of £24.1 billion.[5] Goodwin took early retirement with a pension of £16 million,[6] despite his part in the near collapse of RBS. It needs to be noted that an internal RBS enquiry found no wrong doing in Goodwin's conduct while at the bank, but he does appear to have been rewarded for his failure.

There was the Libor (London Interbank Offered Rate) scandal in London, in which banks conspired to fraudulently report their interest lending rates to profit from trades or to give the impression that they were more creditworthy than they were. Barclays Bank were eventually fined £290 million in June 2012 for their part in the fraud.[7]

Perhaps as a counter-foil to this hypocrisy and greed, the Occupy Wall Street movement began in reaction to the idea that the vast majority of wealth in the world is concentrated in the hands of a minority (1%) of allegedly corrupt, greedy and selfish individuals. This resistance movement of 'the 99%' who "no longer tolerate the greed and corruption of the 1%"[8] provide further evidence of the unbalanced and unethical distribution of economic wealth.

From these countless stories, I can understand why people believe capitalism is evil and all corporations are in some way corrupt. In the case of some businesses, they'd be right. It could be argued that certain businesses do not function as they should but instead do little good and add limited value to their customer; they that aren't really businesses at all. They're not contributing to society in any way and. Quite frankly they're nothing more than a "personal welfare states", making money for the owners or shareholders.

It is this model of business which drives people to protest and occupy Wall Street. It's what drives us a little insane when we call up organisations and get an automated system followed by someone with a long script who doesn't care. It's what makes programmes like *Rogue Traders* and *Watchdog* necessary.

It's what causes 'the 99%' to clamour for change.

Fortunately, these accounts of bad practice taking up the headlines, are only half the story. If you dig a little deeper you'll see that it is far from all bad.

The self-help author John Butcher says, "Capitalism actually works. No other social system can compete with the entrepreneurial free market system in terms of productivity, raising standards of living and creating permanent prosperity. Communism and true socialism simply don't work. They actually hurt people. They've kept entire generations in poverty. They are disastrous though well-meaning systems that have ruined hundreds of millions of lives. Yet somehow there are elements of our culture that still associate profit-making with vice."[9]

It would even be a gross generalisation to suggest that all very wealthy businesses are selfish and driven by greed; many actively work to improve the lives of those less fortunate.

Bill Gates and Warren Buffet have invested billions of their personal fortune into a foundation to tackle some tough challenges: extreme poverty and poor health in developing countries, and the failures of America's education system.[10]

Andrew Carnegie, a steel magnate from the latter half of the nineteenth century, is purported to be responsible for almost every library built in the western world during his lifetime which in turn brought education to the masses.[11]

George and Richard Cadbury were entrepreneurs way ahead of their time who not only established a successful business, but built a whole town to ensure their workers had a healthy and safe place to live. They were ground breaking in their approach to business, giving employees a cash gift to start a pension in 1906 and providing education to all their employees under the age of 18 more than 100 years before the compulsory school leaving age was raised to 18 in England.

And in 1903 Joseph Rowntree took his vast business fortune and created three charitable trusts to improve the lives of his workers and the wider nation with political and social reform. These trusts are still in existence today working to alleviate poverty and improve lives right across the UK.

There is a lot to celebrate about business in light of these philanthropic examples. However, far too often in business, the only mission that is given credence is the mission to increase the turnover and profit forsaking all others!

What if businesses chose not to focus solely on the financial rewards, but instead chose to operate with a more inspiring mission? Is there scope for business to pursue a mission defined by a valuable, caring and outward looking solution which runs alongside a set of laudable core values which define how they intend to behave? What if businesses chose to work for the common good?

Don't get me wrong, businesses should make money. In fact, businesses that don't make money won't last very long. The issue does not lie with a business' monetary success or profitability; shareholders' making a return for taking risks and investing in a growing business. Nor is there anything fundamentally wrong with people being paid well for working hard to build a great business; it makes good business sense to reward talented staff and trusting investors.

The issue which underpins this concept of bad business is mission based on greed - maximising profit at the expense of all other ethical, moral or practical considerations. A business should never be driven solely by a mission "to make as much money as possible." That is pure greed! Greed is what turns capitalism bad. Greed is what causes the subprime mortgage market to collapse. It is what drives Bernie Madoff to steal and what caused thousands of job losses at Enron.

It is, therefore, integral that businesses are founded on excellent core values and with inspiring missions which can be proudly expressed to our customers. Let's build businesses centred on more than just money.

Let's build Communities Of Work (COWs) on a Mission; communities of like-minded people working together to do something great!

Communities of people sharing a vision and creating value not only for themselves but also for their customers and their communities.

Communities of people changing the world!

The aim of this book is to demonstrate that business can be both these things – financially rewarding and ethically and morally centred - if this simple COW model is followed.

This book will help you build your COW!

It will help you define your purpose, gather the right people and create the right culture to win in business with integrity and fulfillment. It will help you build an organisation to change the world.

And, as Jim Collins' has shown in his books *Good To Great* and *Built to Last,* those organisations built on a strong mission and defined by moral values tend to make more money too.

5

PART 1: PURPOSE

An organisational purpose is your north star! It's your guiding light. It explains why your people come to work and defines what they do all day. Your purpose is what pilots your organisation into the future and against which everything your organisation does should be measured.

A purpose gives your team clarity, direction and focus and should be the very heartbeat of your organisation.

With this in mind, the starting point for any business should be to ensure that you can clearly define your organisation's purpose in these three parts:

1. **The mission:** what an organisation does. This is what happens each and every day at the coalface (Google "organises the world's information"; Disney "makes people happy"[12]).

2. **The values:** how an organisation behaves. This defines what is and is not appropriate to do while executing the mission. (For example Zappos aims to - "Be Adventurous, Creative, and Open-Minded; Build a Positive Team and Family Spirit; Be Passionate and Determined; Be humble".)[13]

3. **The vision:** where the organisation is going. The business' vision should be "a big hairy audacious goal"[14] that the organisation aims to achieve. (Amazon Kindle wants to make "Every book ever printed in every language all available in 60 seconds from anywhere on the planet").[15]

Your business' purpose is: what you do, how you do it and where you're going. Let's dig a little deeper into each of these.

2 MISSION

> *"We believe that every organisation has a North Star –*
> *a guiding purpose that remains true over time. Often*
> *the trick is finding that North Star through the haze.*
> *First take the time to locate, describe and define it.*
> *Then help others see that North Star. Only then can*
> *your team navigate by it"*
>
> **Keith Yamashita & Sandra Spataro**[16]

According to dictionary.com a mission statement is "an official document that sets out the purpose and work of an organisation." Simply put, an organisation's mission is what it does. For what purpose do employees start work each and every day? What is it that draws people into the office? When boiled down to a single sentence, what is it that you actually do day in, day out?

Facebook "makes the world more open and connected."

Google "organises the world's information."

Disney "makes people happy."

Ford "provides personal mobility for people around the world."

Walmart "saves people money so that they can live a better life."

Your mission is what you exist for and every organisation has a mission.

Every organisation has a reason why they gather people to a place of work and pay them to do something. Even if you've not thought about it. Even if you've never articulated it or written it down. Even if you've never mentioned it to your workforce, your organisation has a mission.

Keith Yamashita and Sandra Spataro, best-selling authors of *Untsuck*, suggest that there is always a 'North Star' which guides an organisation. They argue that if you don't actively or deliberately define your business' mission, it will define itself; shaped by what the leaders say, how they behave and by what they choose to measure. An organisation at its basic level is nothing more than "a relationship with a purpose"[17] and therefore, simply a group of people that come together to execute a mission.

Whether purposefully defined and overtly expressed or primitively organic and unspoken, your teams will be executing some version of an organisational mission.

However, in order to ensure business growth, building and motivating high performing teams requires people to willingly engage with a common identity; a common understanding and purpose. Teams need to rally round a compelling purpose to become a great team. In my experience, it's best to be in conscious control of that common purpose for your organisation.

So what's *your* mission? What does *your* organisation do? Can you articulate it in a single, simple sentence?

Before you gather your team and start your off site retreat to formalise your mission statement, here's a few helpful tips to remember.

It should be **inspiring**. It needs to appeal to people's emotions. It needs to excite and motivate your teams. It should attract people to it like a moth to a flame.

It should be **short**. It needs to be memorable; more than a couple of sentences and it's too complicated.

It should be **present tense**. If you can't articulate it as if it's happening now then it's not what you do, but instead forms part of your vision.

(It is, perhaps, important to note at this point that there is a distinction between the business' *mission* and its *vision* which should not be confused. I've read many a company mission statement that reads like a vision statement, and the words are often used interchangeably. I will explore vision in more detail in chapter 4, but in essence a mission is what you do and a vision is what you see in the future.)

Now there is an oft told apocryphal story that illustrates the importance of fully understanding your mission. It is about a man who was walking one day, when he came across a building site with three masons who were all working at chipping chunks of granite from large blocks.

The first seemed unhappy at his job, frequently looking at his watch. When the man asked what it was that he was doing, and the mason responded, rather curtly, "I'm hammering this stupid rock, and I can't wait 'til 5 when I can go home."

A second mason, seemingly more interested in his work, was hammering diligently and when asked what it was that he was doing, answered, "Well, I'm moulding this block of rock so that it can be used with others to construct a wall. I'll sure be glad when it's done."

A third mason was hammering at his block fervently, taking time to stand back and admire his work. He chipped off small pieces until he was satisfied that it was the best he could do. When he was questioned about his work he stopped, gazed skyward and proudly proclaimed, "I'm building a cathedral!"

The three different approaches of the stone mason's to their job demonstrates the value of a clearly defined and articulated mission. The first mason merely broke rocks and did not know why; he therefore was disheartened and lacked motivation. In contrast, the third stone mason in our story clearly understood his mission of "creating amazing buildings" and he went about it with enthusiasm and purpose; he used his skills to take part in building amazing edifices. For all three it was the same job. One mission inspires another does not.

Finally a word of warning: mission statements should not be about making money. It is important to differentiate between purpose and necessity. For example, in order to live, humans must breathe; so too businesses need money to thrive. However, oxygen, like money, is a necessity but definitely not the reason for living.

George Merck II, the former head of a global pharmaceutical firm Merck, expressed this notion very well in a speech he made to the Medical College of Virginia in 1950:

> *"We try to remember that medicine is for the patient. We try never to forget that medicine is for the people. It is not for the profits. The profits follow, and if we have remembered that they have never failed to appear. The better we have remembered it, the larger they have been.*
>
> **George Merck II**[18]

If you want to inspire people to build a great organisation focus on the heartbeat of the organisation and not the balance sheet and you'll build something of financial value as well.

So now you have your inspiring, simple mission statement but what about the rules to execute it well? Let's move onto your core values.

3 VALUES

> *"Do all the good you can. By all the means you can. In all the ways you can. In all the places you can. At all the times you can. To all the people you can. As long as ever you can."*
>
> *John Wesley*[19]

An organisation's core values are operating principles that guide internal conduct and relationship with customers, partners, and shareholders. Core values define how a company and its people behave.

For example, Johnson & Johnson say that their "first responsibility is to the doctors, nurses and patients"[20]; a value which was put to the test when a voluntary product recall cost the company $100 million.

Or consider Volvo whose core value is safety. They haven't always produced the best looking cars on the market, but have consistently been on top of the safety rankings.

Notice, that the above definition describes how an organisation *behaves*; not how it *wants to* or *should* behave but how the organisation *actually* behaves.

There are a number of different types of values to consider. Patrick Lencioni, best-selling author, speaker and management consultant, counsels organisations to make a clear distinction between core values, permission to play values and aspirational values.[21]

Core values are the behaviours which a company would go out of business in order to protect; the ones you would not compromise even if it meant the end of your organisation. These are the behaviours that differentiate you from your competitors.

Permission to play values are the core standard by which everybody is required to abide in order to be a part of the organisation. They are simply the minimum standard of behaviour expected and are recognisable across mission statements on a global scale! Character traits like integrity, honesty, respectfulness, communication provide the platform on which all must build.

Aspirational values are those which an organisation aspires to hold. These are the values that maybe need some work and effort to implement across an organisational culture.

This chapter is concerned with the core values of an organisation; those values which are resolutely and uncompromisingly held even in the face of serious consequences.

In order to ascertain your company's core value, you simply need to ask yourself: is there anything you wouldn't do in pursuit of your mission?

But why do we need to define core values? Surely an organisation should be able to employ whatever tactics necessary, within legal parameters, to achieve its mission? Although this hypothesis seems to present a sensible plan of action, research suggests the opposite to be true. It has been argued that having no clear value structure can actually be detrimental to any organisation's long term success.

Francis Fukuyama in *Trust: The Social Virtues and the Creation of Prosperity*, argues that communities that operate from a common value base are able to prosper in adverse circumstances and create wealth out of very little indeed.[22]

Furthermore, Peter Berger, University Professor of Sociology, Emeritus, at Boston University, wrote a series of books that contended that the creation of wealth was not merely an expression of materialism, but that a free economy requires trust and shared values to operate well.[23]

In business, there are a lot of factors which are outside of your control and the landscape changes often and swiftly. Jim Collins asserts in *Good to Great* that the key to building a successful organisation is to hold a very clear understanding of its immutable core values and preserve these at all costs. Any changes to the rest of the organisation can be made in line with the ever changing requirements of the market without impinging on its core principles.

In essence, if an organisation wants to become great, it must recognise which aspects need to change with the moving economies and what must never be changed. It must "preserve the core and stimulate progress."[24]

The story of J. Urwin Miller is a wonderful illustration of core values in action.

In 1934 Miller become the General Manager of the Cummins Engine Company, which was founded by his great uncle to design, build and service power technologies. Nearly 80 years later, it is a Fortune 500 company operating in 160 countries across the world, with nearly $10 billion in turnover.

Miller, a committed Christian, was motivated to approach business as a form of discipleship, acting with integrity and honesty. In the 1930s, Miller supported the formation of a union at his organisation, Cummins, which was contrary to popular business practice at the time and long before he was asked. Later, in the 1970s Miller acted with integrity when he chose to shut down operations in South Africa in reaction to the government's ruling which would not allow a racially integrated workforce. Miller even encouraged the company to extend benefits to domestic partners of employees, at vast expense to the company[25] when no one else expected it.

Behaving so altruistically probably incurred great personal cost for Miller and it certainly cost Cummins Engine Company, but it was also non-negotiable; a core value which he would not compromise on.

What are the things that you will not compromise on in the pursuit of your mission? What are the three or four things that other people outside your organisation always say about you? What are the things that define you as an organisation? It is these qualities which are your core values.

Try to keep your core values to three or four and make them a single short sentence each. Just like the missions – **short, easy to remember** and in the **present tense**.

For example, Cogiva's core values are:

Honour God: we honour God in all we do.

Love what we do: we work hard with passion, enthusiasm and commitment; having fun while doing good.

Try new things: we expect and make room for people to think creatively, take risks and make mistakes.

These are things at the heart of what Cogiva does and we will not compromise on them – if we stop having fun then we will stop doing business. We won't work with organisations that we are not passionate about. There will never be punishment for a mistake made for the right reasons. We are really clear about what we will and will not do in pursuit of our mission.

If you want to build a missional business to change the world *you* need to be clear about what you will and will not do in pursuit of *your* mission. It's the most effective way to get to where you want to go as an organisation.

> *'Having a simple set of values for a company was also a very efficient and expedient way to go…Because if*

somebody makes a proposal and it infringes on those values, you don't study it for two years. You just say, "No, we don't do that." And you go on quickly.'

Herb Kelleher[26]

But where do you want to go? What's your vision?

4 VISION

"In real life, strategy is actually very straight forward.
You pick a general direction and implement like hell"

Jack Welch[27]

The definition of vision is 'the act or power of anticipating that which will come to be; a vivid, imaginative conception or anticipation.' A vision is a picture of what your organisation will be or do in future.

For example, Amazon Kindle wants to make "Every book ever printed in every language all available in 60 seconds from anywhere on the planet." Nike aims "to bring inspiration and innovation to every athlete in the world."

Your vision is an exciting and challenging view of your organisation's future.

In the previous chapter we mentioned Jim Collins' admonition to "preserve the core and stimulate progress." One of the key ways he encourages organisations to do this is with what he calls a "BHAG" or "A Big Hairy Audacious Goal."[28]

A BHAG is a vision that falls into the grey area of what might be possible and what seems impossible. It doesn't just inspire people, it challenges them to be more than they ever believed possible. A well-articulated vision grabs people on an emotional level, drawing them into be part of something bigger than themselves.

In his speech to Rice University in September 1962, President Kennedy set the ultimate BHAG saying, "We choose to go to the moon in this decade and do the other things not because they are easy, but because they are hard, because that goal will serve to organize and measure the best of our energies and skills, because that challenge is one that we are willing to accept, one we are unwilling to postpone, and one which we intend to win."[29]

"Put a man on the moon!" Now that's a great vision!

Moreover, in August 1914 Sir Ernest Shackleton[30] set sail on the *Endurance* to take a team to the South Pole. Just one day away from their intended destination the ship got stuck fast in the ice and was eventually crushed, leaving the men to camp on an ice floe for 18 months. Ravaged by Antarctic storms, twelve hundred miles from the nearest civilisation, Shackleton abandoned his original vision of reaching the South Pole in favour of an even more implausible vision: to get everyone of his men home alive.

Shackleton choose to take a small crew in a twenty foot lifeboat and attempt the treacherous trip of 800 miles across the most stormy stretch of ocean in the world facing fifty foot waves.

On the 17 August 1917, Shackleton returned and rescued his entire crew; not a single person was lost.

Now that's a BHAG! An almost impossible vision of the future that rallies people to achieve above and beyond what they ever thought possible.

A compelling vision also allows you to regulate what projects and activities the organisation gets involved in. You can have the most compelling vision, but if the workforce is not united to the same end, it will never come to fruition.

It's a well-known fact in sport that no matter how good your individual team players are, no matter how skilled or experienced your personnel, a team will never win a championship if the individuals on the team are working to different agendas.

Whether its sports or business, your team need to be pulling in the same direction to win. The most productive way of ensuring this is by having a clearly defined and comprehensively understood vision.

That's what a great vision does - it focuses, inspires , gathers and challenges people.

To do that a vision needs to be three things:

Almost out of reach: a good vision is far enough away that it is a challenge, but close enough that people can see that it just might be possible.

Short: people should be able to easily remember it. Like the mission, if it's more than a couple of sentences, it's too complicated.

Inspiring: it needs to evoke an emotional response and be something that people can connect with on more than a rational level, if they are to put time, energy and heart into making it real.

One of best examples of an inspiring vision is from Oxfam, the international charity which sees the future as "a just world without poverty."[31] It's short, memorable, easy to understand, evokes an emotive response that draws me in and most importantly it is big, very, very big!

So what is it that your organisation is going to do? How do you see the future 10 years from now? What's your moon shot?

PART 2: PEOPLE

In the early 1980s, the Ford Motor Company was not enjoying its previously heady success. It was losing money - $3.3 billion over three years[32] – to its cheaper and more efficient Japanese competitors. But Ford didn't panic. In 1983 they set about restoring the fortunes of the 80 year old motor company.

The first step made by the management team was to clarify exactly what it was that Ford Motor Company stood for; they began redefining the mission, values and guiding principles (a document that later become known as MVGP).

However, during this process they discovered something that had been overlooked by the organisation. Something which had been at the heart of Henry Ford's founding vision. Don Peterson, the former CEO, recalls that "there was a great deal of talk about the sequence of the three Ps – people, products and profits. It was decided that people should absolutely come first."[33]

Getting the right people "on the bus"[34], as Jim Collins puts it, is vitally important to the success of your organisation. Often, even a slight change in the composition of your team can make a radical difference in its ability to perform.[35]

Whether good or bad, people will impact your organisation's ability to execute its mission and it's imperative to get the right people.

> *"Any strategy, no matter how smart, is dead on arrival unless a company brings it to life with people – the right people."*
>
> *Jack Welch*[36]

But who are the right people?

5 CATCH THE VISION

> *"There are many things that will catch my eye, but there are only a few things that will catch my heart."*

Tim Redmond[37]

If you start your career when you're 21 and work through to the current UK retirement age of 65, you will work for 44 years. For each year that you work, you will spend about 228 days in the office, which equates to more than 10,000 days in your lifetime. At a standard eight hours a days, that's over 80,000 hours of work. That's an awful lot of hours of your life to invest in something.

Would you rather invest all that time into something that captures your heart, or something that merely pays well? I know which I would choose!

Daniel Pink in his book *Drive*, describes a series of experiments which uncovered an interesting phenomenon. For any task other than a purely repetitive, unskilled task, financial reward actually has an adverse impact on performance.[38] In essence, the more you offer in terms of reward, the worse the person's performance gets. It seems that the pressure to *have to* perform actually undermines a person's ability to perform.

Put simply, you can't make someone do a task well just for monetary compensation. So, if you can't get the best from a person by simply paying them more, how do you get a team to perform to their peak?

Obviously you need to give them some other reason to do what you're asking. You need to appeal to their emotions. You need to capture their heart with a compelling and challenging picture of the future. You need to give their work meaning with a mission that inspires them.

Ultimately, you need them to catch your vision.

In *The 8th Habit*, Stephen Covey suggests that we all desire to have unique personal significance; what Covey calls voice.[39] Our voice, which motivates us to a higher level of performance, occurs when four things come together: our passion, our talent, our need and our conscience. Satisfying need alone, with financial reward, is not sufficient to inspire us to do our best work.

To truly do great work we must release our passion (that which energises and inspires us); we must appeal to our conscience (that small, internal voice that assures us we are doing good); and we must employ our talent (that which we were born to do).

James Stillman, president of Citicorp at the turn of the last century, fully understood the benefits of gathering a team that were passionate about a shared vision:

> *"Stillman intended [Citicorp] to retain its position [as the largest and strongest bank in the US] even after his death, and to ensure this he filled the new building with people who shared his own vision and entrepreneurial spirit."*
>
> **Citibank 1812 – 1970[40]**

James Stillman built an institution that could continue without him and more than 100 years later Citigroup (a successor to Citicorp) sits at number 20 on the Fortune 500 list, with a 4% increase in profits in 2011. Not too shabby for a bank during a recession!

But not all organisations have a leader like Stillman. A Gallup poll in the U.S. taken in 2011 showed that 71% of workers were emotionally disengaged from their workplace and as a result, were less productive[41] which, Gallup estimated, cost businesses a staggering $350 billion every year; that's $2,246 per disengaged employee.[42]

That figure doesn't even take into account the impact a single disengaged employee has on the culture of an organisation. After all, misery is contagious!

The key thing about vision is that you can't teach it. You can't train someone to be passionate about your vision. You can't pay them to see what you can see. You can run a weekend retreat and get people fired up. You can deliver a rousing speech and inspire people, but you can't create a long term, day-in-day-out connection with a vision through training.

People either connect or they don't. So don't waste your money, hire people in the first instance that already catch the vision.

Edward Deci, a university psychology graduate student in 1969, wrote that people have an "inherent tendency to seek out novelty and challenges, to extend and exercise their capabilities, to explore, and to learn." If you can give employees a compelling vision in which to exercise that 'inherent tendency', then you will be surprised what someone will achieve and you will save yourself time, effort and money in having to manage and organise them. (But we'll get to all that in part 3.)

For instance, consider Valve, a game development company with an extremely flat management structure. According to their handbook for new employees, subtitled, "A fearless adventure in knowing what to do when no one's there telling you what to do"[43], there is no hierarchy.

> *When you're an entertainment company that's spent the last decade going out of its way to recruit the most intelligent, innovative, talented people on Earth, telling them to sit at a desk and do what they're told obliterates 99 percent of their value. We want innovators, and that means maintaining an environment where they'll flourish... This company is yours to steer– toward opportunities and away from risks.*
>
> **Valve Handbook**[44]

The future of the company is directly in the hands of the people they hired. People that catch the vision. People that have built Valve up to a $2 billion company.[45]

People that catch the vision are your best asset. Once you're sure they see what you see, make sure they fit the culture.

6 FIT THE CULTURE

A culture may be conceived as a network of beliefs and purposes in which any string in the net pulls and is pulled by the others, thus perpetually changing the configuration of the whole.

Jacques Barzun[46]

Imagine, you invited someone to your house for dinner. You set the table: cutlery, crockery, wine glasses. You devised and crafted a delicious menu: starter, main course and homemade desert. Your guest arrives and you all sit down to eat. Then things get interesting.

Your guest starts eating with his hands, shovelling food in like a starving animal, and he talks constantly even with his mouth full. Conversation doesn't flow, it's a monologue, and the language your visitor is using has never been uttered before in your house.

How would you feel?

I know it would make me quite uncomfortable. I'm not sure I would know what to do. Should I ignore him, be polite, finish dinner quickly and usher him out of the house, remembering never to invite him again? Should I say something and try to address the behaviour?

The issue is that I've created a culture in my house (it may not be explicit, but it's there: standards of behaviour, expectations of how we speak, the etiquette of politeness) and when it's violated, it causes problems. When someone comes in and cuts across that culture, the atmosphere becomes quite strained.

And so it is within your organisation.

Organisational culture is a system of shared values and beliefs about what's important and appropriate in an organisation; values and beliefs that are widely shared and reflected in the daily practices.[47]

Whether you've deliberately created your culture or it has organically grown by default, it will be an intrinsic and very evident part of your company. Inviting someone into this environment who does not share the same cultural values and beliefs will cause friction, in the same way as a rude dinner guest would in your house.

Just as one bad apple spoils the batch, so one person that does not choose to accept and live by an organisation's values can undermine the entire culture and atmosphere, unsettling the rest of your team.

I mentioned early that you need to ensure that people in your organisation catch the vision. You also need to ensure that people share the values too; that they are happy behaving as you would want them to behave.

You need to ensure that they fit your culture.

It takes a lot of effort and time to build an organisational culture. Don't risk disrupting it, no matter how skilled or talented a prospective employee appears, if they don't fit the culture, don't hire them.

When Jack Welch was CEO of General Electric, he presided over a team of leaders who grew the organisation by 4000%, in multiple markets across the globe. He knew a thing or two about hiring the right kind of people.

In his book *Winning*, Jack clearly outlines the framework that he used to decide whether or not a person was suitable to work at GE. The framework assessed a person in eight areas: integrity, intelligence, maturity, energy, energising others, courage, ability to execute and passion.[48]

The unusual thing about this list, especially in light of the world class nature of the organisation, is that only two out of the eight areas relate to skill – intelligence and ability to execute. The other six are all related to the person's character. Seventy five percent of Jack's selection process focused on discovering who a person was rather than what they could do; he was clearly more concerned to discover whether a person would fit the organisation's culture.

According to Edgar Schein, a professor at MIT Sloan School of Management, "The only thing of real importance that leaders do is to create and manage culture."[49] Whether or not you agree that it's the *only* thing a leader does, it is certainly one of the most important aspects of leadership. Moreover, one thing a leader does need to do is ensure that nothing interferes with the culture they want to foster within the organisation.

Herb Kelleher, founder of Southwest Airlines, believed that you should hire primarily for character and attitude rather than skill. He always maintained that once you had the right person, you could always train them to improve their skill[50] but it's nearly impossible to change a person's character; to mould them to the inherent culture is difficult and takes time and effort.

Be deliberate about building your culture and hire people with the character that fits.

Take a lead from Zappos, the billion dollar online shoe retailer. Zappos are so fervent about ensuring they employ the right people, that one week into their 4 week induction, they offer each new employee $2000 to quit there and then. It may sound excessive, but it ensures that they only get people that want to work for them and it protects the culture that Tony Hseih, the CEO, has meticulously crafted.

In order to build a missional business that changes the world, you must protect your culture at all costs and to do this well you will also need just the right leaders.

7 LEADERS

> *"If you can't influence others they won't follow you.*
> *And if they won't follow you, you're not a leader."*
>
> **Jack Welch**[51]

In his best-selling book, *The 21 Irrefutable Laws of Leadership*, John Maxwell recalls a sobering but extremely visual demonstration of leadership: "Occasionally," he writes "you hear of four military jets crashing while flying in formation." Maxwell explains that when jet fighters fly in formation, one of the pilots is designated the leader. The leader defines everything: where the formation flies; what altitude they fly at; what speed they fly at; what maneuvers they perform. Whatever maneuvers the leader makes the other planes flying on his wing also make: "This is true whether he soars in the clouds or crashes into a mountaintop."[52]

Any way you look at it, leaders will have a profound effect on the success or failure of an organisation; "Everything rises and falls on leadership."[53] The leaders bring an organisation to life and for better or for worse your leaders colour your whole organisation, so choose them very carefully.

Firstly, recognise that leadership is not about title or position in an organisation. Leadership is simply about influence. As Jack Welch puts it, "if you can't influence others they won't follow you. And if they won't follow you, you're not a leader."[54] Good leaders know this. They don't hold their position highly, but they do protect their relationships with integrity and loyalty.

Make sure your leaders are people who can build and maintain relationships well. If necessary get rid of titles and hierarchy, true leaders do not need them to successfully lead.

> *"Being in power is like being a lady. If you have to tell people you are, you aren't"*
>
> *Margaret Thatcher*[55]

Secondly, great leaders are able to build and engender trust. Trust turns a good team into a great team. Where there is genuine trust, a team can work unfettered by the shadow of organisational politics; agendas do not need to be questioned; information does not get hoarded; people are free to excel in their own sphere and to work together for the common good.

Great leaders can create that trust within a team and take a group of individuals of average skill to the level of a high performing team.

Take the Greek football team, who in 2004 achieved what is probably still the biggest shock in football, beating the favoured hosts, Portugal to win the European Championship. Greece was a team of average players without a single household name, taking on the might of Cristiano Ronaldo and Luis Figo, who was, at the time, the most expensive footballer in the world. But what Otto Rehhagel, the Greek coach managed to do was get a group of average individuals to play above themselves as a high performing team, beating a much more skilled group of world class individuals.

One of the key ways that leaders build trust is by serving. Great leaders are able to subordinate their ego for the greater good: "It's not that [they] have no ego or self-interest. Indeed, they are incredibly ambitious – but their ambition is first and foremost for the institution, not themselves."[56]

The leaders you are looking for have the strength to surround themselves with people smarter and more skilled than they are themselves, people that know better. They are not intimidated by other people's success or ability. They are able to put their whole focus on doing everything they can to make sure their team can perform and succeed.

> *"The best executive is the one who has the sense enough to pick good men to do what he wants done and the self-restraint enough to keep from meddling with them while they do it."*
>
> **Theodore Roosevelt[57]**

As one longtime employee at Hewlett Packard put it, "I have the impression that Bill [Hewlett] and Dave [Packard] work for me, rather than the other way around."[58] And, Nordstrom the clothing retailer, has an organisational chart that's an upside down pyramid with the board of directors at the bottom, serving the staff, who serve the customer.[59]

Thirdly, great leaders live and breathe the mission, vision and values of an organisation and by this they set the culture and expectations within the organisation.

Every person in your organisation must be infused with the company DNA; they must grasp and live out the mission and vision of the organisation, but the leaders are the ones that make that happen. For them it must become a mantra; a constant CD on single track repeat. They must return to it regularly; they must communicate it in all interactions – verbally and non-verbally; they must become the living embodiment of the mission, values and vision of the organisation. In doing so, people *will* copy them.

Jack Welch believes that the formation of the mission, vision and values of the organisation can only be set by the leadership. It cannot be delegated and must come from the leadership. It must be part of who they are as individuals and as a leadership team.[60]

Like the rest of your team, leaders must catch the vision; they must fit the culture, but they are a special breed. When hiring leaders you should look for people who don't care for title, who build trust and who are almost as maniacal about the mission, values and vision of your organisation as you are!

Choose your leaders wisely, they play a big part in developing the 'props' of your organisation.

PART 3: PROPS

Once you have your mission, vision and values established, it is important that you take time to ensure that this purpose and the underlying values permeate every area of your business: from how you talk to each other in the office, to the physical space that your customers see; from the metrics you measure to the structure and teams you create; from the processes you write to the remuneration you offer. This ensures you create your Community of Work, founded on integrity and established with potential for real and lasting success.

Everything flows from this what, why and where to!

I've mentioned already that every organisation has a mission, core values and vision; whether they are explicit and deliberately cultivated or left to organically develop. Every organisation's purpose and culture is expressed through the collective actions of its teams not through words in a corporate document.

Even if you have spent hours defining and articulating what you believe your mission, values and vision to be, unless they are lived out in the behaviours and attitudes of the people in your organisation, they are nothing more than wishful thinking. The truly active purpose of your organisation is cultivated through developing the right systems and environment to establish behaviours and attitudes that match your aspirations.

We have all seen organisations that espouse a very laudable purpose, yet seem to struggle to live it out at the coalface! Unless you are deliberate about designing your metrics and rewards; your policies and procedures; your environment to express and reflect your very core values and mission, your organisation will fail to deliver on its articulated 'raison d'etre'. In short, it will be inauthentic. Don't let that happen. Be as deliberate about the functional parts of your organisation as you have been about the purpose and people.

8 METRICS & REWARDS

> *"The purpose of compensation should not be to get the right behaviours from the wrong people, but to get the right people on the bus in the first place and keep them there."*
>
> *Jim Collins*[61]

I once heard a story about a consultant who was invited into a large organisation to work with their sales team. The sales director had asked for the consultant's help. His team was performing reasonably well, but he felt if they would only work together more, their results would improve massively. He had tried many ways to motivate his team into collaborating better, but all to no avail.

"I don't know what I'm missing, but I don't seem to be able to get them to support each other," he said to the consultant.

The consultant sat and listened to the sales director while looking around his well-appointed office. Suddenly, he noticed a large chart on the wall behind the director's desk. On it were pictures of all his sales staff and a beautiful picture of a golden beach in Bermuda.

"What's that?" the consultant asked.

The sales director smiled proudly and said "that's the league table of each salesman's performance. The best performing salesman wins a trip to Bermuda at the end of the year."

It seems fairly obvious when hearing this story that while his team are competing against each other for a trip to Bermuda, they're never going to help each other. This sales director was never going to get his team to collaborate until he changed what he measured and what he rewarded.

However, it's not so obvious to identify in most organisations. I've seen this phenomenon many times in more subtle ways – companies articulating a laudable mission and inspiring core values only to undermine them with their systems of management information and compensation.

Jim Collins' study in *Good to Great* found that a lot of organisations have great intentions and inspiring visions but not only fail to translate this intention into a concrete strategy, they even tolerate tactics, characteristics and strategies that push against their mission and values.[62]

Your metrics, rewards and incentives must be fully aligned with the purpose and values and designed to encourage the culture you're creating.

If incentives are all geared towards individual reward, then who's going to co-operate? If they are all directed at delivering the monthly sales numbers, will anyone act for the longer term goals? If you measure working hours, but not quality and volume of work, people will be on time and possibly work long hours, but are unlikely to deliver their best work.

Quite simply, building your mission, vision and values as we discussed in section one, is a total waste of time unless it is backed up by organisational practices that put them at the heart of the organisation. In order to make the mission, vision and values the heart of an organisation, you must build the metrics and rewards around them.

Firstly, whatever management information you decide you need to effectively run your organisation, should be designed to inform you whether or not you are working out your mission; how consistent you are with your core values and demonstrate whether you are moving towards your vision.

Secondly, whatever compensation, benefit and system of praise you implement should reward those people who execute the mission well and espouse the values. Moreover, it should sanction those who contravene the values and fail to work towards the vision.

To put it simply, what you measure, the behaviours you praise and the behaviours you punish will become your culture.[63]

Furthermore, your reward system should not just about financial gain. In his book *Building a Happiness Centred Business*, Paddi Lund an Australian Dentist, reminds us that "those acts motivated by emotional rewards are most consistently performed."[64] You can choose to be very creative with your system of recognition and rewards. For example, you might try more flexible working; or leaving hand written notes on your teams' desks; maybe organise special events; give high performers surprise and random extra days off; give out monopoly money that can be exchanged for gifts and treats.

Whatever works for your people, as long as it constantly reiterates the mission, values and vision of your organisation.

It should also be non-bureacratic[65], which brings us to 'polices and procedures.'

9 POLICIES & PROCEDURE

> *"Relentlessly seek out the best practices to achieve your big d*×*ha [vision], whether inside or out, adapt them and continually improve them."*
>
> *Jack Welch*[66]

If you were writing a handbook for new recruits at your organisation, what would it include? How big would it be? How many *dos* and *don'ts* would it contain? Would it match the official one that your organisation gives to new starters?

For many years, new recruits at Nordstrom, an American upscale fashion retailer, were given a simple 5-by-8-inch card containing just 75 words:

> *"Welcome to Nordstrom*
>
> *We're glad to have you with our Company. Our number one goal is to provide outstanding customer service. Set both your personal and professional goals high. We have great confidence in your ability to*

achieve them.

Nordstrom Rules: Rule #1: Use best judgment in all situations. There will be no additional rules.

Please feel free to ask your department manager, store manager, or division general manager any question at any time. [67]

At Nordstrom, employees aren't just given responsibility, they are given authority too. They are given permission to do their job within the confines of the Nordstrom mission and values to provide outstanding customer service, but they are free to decide how best to do their job.

This is the heart of what it means to build a C.O.W on a mission. A community of like-minded people with a passion, freed to be brilliant at what they do. But it's not easy to accomplish.

At the turn of the nineteenth century, the world was based around an agricultural economy. Farmers had livestock and grew produce, trading them nationally and globally. Then, during the nineteenth century, all that changed and the world moved into the industrial age. Factories sprung up, manufacturing thrived and people moved from the fields to the cities.

During the Industrial Age, the key to success was efficiency and the most valuable assets were the means of production – the expensive machines. People were needed to operate the machines, but not to think or make decisions. All they needed to do was simply follow the prescribed procedures. People were a resource, but they were not assets.

Since then we have moved into the Information Age, where people are the means of production. People are now valuable assets and need to be released to produce. However, many organisations still work to the paradigm of the Industrial Age, where workers are nothing more than resources who follow instructions. Unfortunately, this system will no longer produce the best results.[68] Like Nordstrom, organisations need to recognise their workers as assets and set them free to perform.

As Theodore Malloch points out "critics of capitalism in the last century did not deny that the industrial revolution had drastically increased wealth, but that it had reduced individuals to an impersonal cog in the wealth machine."[69]

Too many policies and procedures make this a reality, with people reduced to cogs or simple resources in the HR database.

Jack Welch shares a conversation he had with one employee who told him "for twenty five years you paid for my hands when you could have had my brain as well – for nothing."[70]

The alternative is much simpler. Hire the right people and trust them to do what needs to be done, without having to resort to creating reams of regulating policies and procedures.

Jim Nordstrom, CEO and the grandson of Nordstrom's founder, was once questioned in a Stanford Business School class about what his staff would do if a customer attempted to return a dress that had clearly been worn. His answer sums up what it means to employ the right people and cut them loose to do the right thing with authority and responsibility:

> *"I don't know. That's the honest answer. But I do*
> *have a high level of confidence that...the customer*
> *would feel well treated and served...We view our*
> *people as sales professionals. They don't need rules.*
> *They need basic guideposts, but not rules. You can do*
> *anything you need to at Nordstrom to get the job done,*
> *just so long as you live up to our basic values and*
> *standards.*
>
> **Jim Nordstrom**[71]

Richard Branson reiterates this notion, "All you can do is hire the right people and empower them to sort things out as they happen."[72]

If you have employed the right people and the right leaders; if you have the right metrics and rewards in place, you shouldn't need vast amounts of policies.

Nevertheless, whatever policies and procedures you do implement, just like the metrics and rewards, should consistently and constantly reinforce the mission, values and vision of your organisation. Put simply: implement the fewest possible policies and procedures necessary to make it easy for your team to exercise their role well and meet their responsibilities.

Avoid bureaucracy at all costs. Bureaucracy is merely to compensate for incompetence and lack of discipline.[73]

10 SPACE & ENVIRONMENT

> *"We don't have a lot of time on this earth⊠We weren't meant to spend it this way. Human beings were not meant to sit in little cubicles staring at computer screens all day."*
>
> **Peter Gibbons** [74]

The Facebook offices still have bare walls and unfinished internal decor. Google has slides, a dinosaur and no one is allowed to be more than 100 metres from food.[75] Red Bull's London office is designed to feel more like a lounge- and the reception turns into a bar at night. Zappos, the online shoe retailer, has stuck to office cubicles, but encourages each and every employee to customise their space with decorations, toys and trinkets. Staff at Value, the games developer, all have desks on wheels.

These global companies and many more besides, spend hundreds of millions of pounds every year to ensure their work spaces are fun, inspiring and foster productivity. The work environment of your organisation matters.

If you're booking a holiday would you choose a hotel with bare fluorescent lighting in the room; no windows at all; all the walls and furnishings the same colour – grey? Grey walls, grey bed, grey curtains, grey carpet! Of course you wouldn't, because it wouldn't be a very relaxing and uplifting holiday. The space you are in hugely influences your mood and by extension your actions.

The design of your workspace has a massive impact on your teams' productivity and is a useful daily influence to reinforce the mission, vision and values of your organisation. Good spaces that are well-designed can become the means by which your organisation can accelerate the achievement of its aims.[76]

Facebook's unfinished spaces are a constant remind to employees that Facebook is always a work in progress.

Value's desks on wheels enables employs to move to whatever team they want to work in, consistent with their culture of choice.

Zappos daily reinforces their value that the company *is* the employees by having them design the spaces.

And Google...well who doesn't love a slide!

Researchers have found that effectively designed office environments can inspire creativity and help people to focus their attention. Even the colour of the walls can make a big difference. Test-takers in this research who were surrounded by red walls were better at skills requiring accuracy and attention to detail, while workers in blue environments were more creative. People who worked in high-ceiling rooms were significantly better at seeing the connections between seemingly unrelated subjects.[77]

The Ambius study references a PhD thesis at the University of Exeter that found enriched work environments improve productivity by around 15%. Not just that, but giving office workers a say in the design upped productivity by 30%.[78]

We've already mentioned the importance of your people to the organisation and having a well-designed and inspiring work place can help by attracting and keeping the right people. If your spaces reflect who you are (your values) and what you're trying to do (your mission and vision) then the right people will naturally feel at home and want to join you.

Daniel Keighron-Foster, CEO of Melbourne, a server hosting company, says "while it may seem a frivolous expense, the idea is to make it impossible for someone to want to leave. If you look at the costs of bringing on a new person, recruitment, months before they're fully productive, the additional cost of the office is easily outweighed."[79]

In the same way you have been deliberate about how you reward and the way you implement procedures, do not leave your spaces to evolve; be deliberate about designing them. Think about how your space reflects your values as an organisation. Decide how you want to use the space to daily reinforce your mission. Find ways to keep the vision of the company regularly in people's consciousness.

Think about what work actually needs to be done in the space. Do people need to collaborate? Do you need to provide spaces where people can be on their own? Do you need space for people just to talk?

Kevin Kuske, General Manager of Turnstone Furniture Maker, advises that businesses create zones; "if I want to talk, I stand at the kitchen counter because that's where everyone comes and talks. If I need some privacy, I find two couches pulled together."[80]

Similarly, Skype, the internet phone company, nurtures collaboration by having workers sit at benches that allow for an easy exchange of ideas. Yet, headphones are the respected way of signaling "leave me alone, I'm thinking," and the company also offers a variety of small, private places for individuals who need quiet and less stimulation.

Whatever your organisation is trying to achieve, having the right space is vitally important; too important to leave to chance! When you've spent valuable time crafting your mission and defining your systems, don't undermined them with badly designed space.

11 FINAL THOUGHTS

> *"Frankly, integrity is just the ticket to the game. If you don't have it in your bones, you shouldn't be allowed on the field."*
>
> *Jack Welch* [81]

Capitalism is not bad in and of itself. In 1970, 76% of the world's poor lived in Asia with only 11% living in Africa. However by 1998, through economic growth, China and India successfully lifted so many people from poverty that those statistics almost reversed with only 15% of the world's poor residing in Asia whilst 66% were in Africa.[82]

However, as a number of studies have shown, profit-at–all-costs is a dangerous aspiration. It is pure and simple greed and by aiming directly for it, businesses will often lose that which they were chasing.

Theodore Malloch sums it up very well when he writes that though a company's well being relies on profit:

"...by seeking at all costs to be profitable, we destroy the conditions on which profitability depends. We alienate our workforce or the local community, we destroy incentive and undermine the workplace as a forum for communal life, we become locked in old and once profitable ways long after the competition has made them unprofitable, and so on. The story has been told many times and in many ways. But the essence is simple: success in a market economy does not come because you aim at it; success comes because you have found your ecological niche and can flourish there by doing your own valuable thing. And doing your own thing must have a social, moral and spiritual dimension if it is to attract the loyalty and commitment of the people with whom and for whom you do it."

Theodore Roosevelt Malloch [83]

Choose to build a missional business:

Found your organisation on an inspiring mission; operate with non-negotiable values; drive towards a 'big hairy audacious' vision; journey with people that share your vision and fit your culture; recruit the help of truly great leaders; reward people according to your purpose; manage and lead according to your values; live and behave how you expect others to...

...and go change the world!

If you would like help to develop and articulate your organisation's mission, values and vision you can contact Ben in any of the following ways:

www.cogiva.com
email: ben@cogiva.com
Twitter: @Cogiva
Facebook: /Cogiva

ABOUT THE AUTHOR

Favourite Book: *Oh the places you'll go* by Dr Seuss.
Favourite Place: Two Bridges on Dartmoor.
Favourite Film: *Gattaca* by Andrew Nichol / *Clue* by Jon Lynn
Little Know Fact: I hate jelly. Really don't see the point!

Husband of one, father of three, real ale lover, rugby watcher, avid reader and uber geek.

Ben has a passion to inspire, motivate, excite and challenge organisations to be brilliant. He wants to encourage business to be built on a foundation of inspiring mission, honest core values and an audacious vision.

Ben Drury is an entrepreneur, a very experienced coder and trained social worker. He understands people and cultures and is a dynamic, entertaining and innovative speaker, who has honed his skills during 15 years involvement in stage productions.

He has worked touring with theatre companies, designing internet banks, writing and directing stage productions, developing and delivering leadership training courses, managing small businesses, building web applications and developing social media strategies.

He now lives at the coast in the North East of England with his wife and three children, watching rugby, writing and speaking.

To find out more and book Ben, visit **www.cogiva.com**.

ENDNOTES

1 Richard Branson (2008). Business Stripped Bare: Adventures of a global entrepreneur. London: Random House. p16.
2 "Wife Says She and Madoff Tried Suicide". The New York Times. Reuters. October 26, 2011.
3 Voreacos, David; Glovin, David (December 13, 2008). "Madoff Confessed $50 Billion Fraud Before FBI Arrest". Bloomberg News.
4 RBS et mon droit: HM deficits FT Alphaville. Retrieved 20 January 2009.
5 The Guardian, 26 February 2009, RBS record losses raise prospect of 95% state ownership
6 The Daily Telegraph, 26 February 2009, Sir Fred Goodwin refuses to return pension
7 BBC. (2012). Timeline: Libor-fixing scandal. Available: http://www.bbc.co.uk/news/business-18671255. Last accessed 21st July 2013.
8 Occupy Wall Street Website (2013) Available: http://occupywallst.org/. Last accessed 21st July 2013.
9 Richard Branson. (2008). In defence of capitalism. Available: http://www.dailymail.co.uk/news/article-1061463/In-defence-capitalism-Richard-Branson-argues-free-markets-enrich-gives-tips-YOU-success.html. Last accessed 22nd July 2013.
10 Gates Foundation. (2013). Gates. Available: http://www.gatesfoundation.org/Who-We-Are/General-Information/Leadership/Management-Committee. Last accessed 22nd July 2013.
11 Richard Branson (2008). Business Stripped Bare: Adventures of a global entrepreneur. London: Random House. p39.
12 Google. (1998). Google. Available: http://www.google.co.uk/about/company/. Last accessed 22nd July 2013.
13 Zappos. (2013). Zappos Family Core Values. Available: http://about.zappos.com/our-unique-culture/zappos-core-values. Last accessed 22nd July 2013.
14 Jim Collins & Jerry I. Porras (2005). Built to Last: Successful Habits

of Visionary Companies. London: Random House. P89.

15 Ken Clark. (2009). The Kindle Vision Statement. Available: http://www.nineboxes.net/2009/12/the-kindle-vision-statement/. Last accessed 22nd July 2013.

16 Keith Yamashita & Sandra Spataro (2004). Unstuck. New York: Portfolio. p125.

17 Stephen R Covey (2004). The 8th Habit: From Effectiveness to Greatness. London: Simon & Schuster. p99.

18 Jim Collins & Jerry I. Porras (2005). Built to Last: Successful Habits of Visionary Companies. London: Random House. p48.

19 Good Reads. (2013). John Wesley Quotes. Available: http://www.goodreads.com/quotes/12757-do-all-the-good-you-can-by-all-the-means. Last accessed 22nd July 2013.

20 Allison Canty. (2010). Core Values and the Companies That Do Them Well. Available: http://grasshopper.com/blog/2010/04/core-values-and-the-companies-that-do-them-well/. Last accessed 22nd July 2013.

21 Patrick Lencioni. (2013). Make Your Values Mean Something. Available: http://www.tablegroup.com/pat/articles/article/?id=20. Last accessed 22nd July 2013.

22 Francis Fukuyama (1996). Trust: The Social Virtues and the Creation of Prosperity. New York: Free Press Paperbacks.

23 Theodore Roosevelt Malloch (2008). Virtuous Business. Nashville: Thomas Nelson. p3.

24 Jim Collins & Jerry I. Porras (2005). Built to Last: Successful Habits of Visionary Companies. London: Random House. p89.

25 Theodore Roosevelt Malloch (2008). Virtuous Business. Nashville: Thomas Nelson. p89.

26 Max Nisen. (2013). Southwest's Founder Explains Why There's No Secret Behind Its Great Culture. Available: http://www.businessinsider.com/southwests-founder-discusses-its-culture-2013-1. Last accessed 30th July 2013.

27 Jack Welch & Suzy Welch (2005). Winning. London: Harper Collins. p165.

28 Jim Collins & Jerry I. Porras (2005). Built to Last: Successful Habits of Visionary Companies. London: Random House. p89.

29 John F. Kennedy. (2012). John F. Kennedy Moon Speech - Rice Stadium. Available: http://er.jsc.nasa.gov/seh/ricetalk.htm. Last accessed 22nd July 2013.

30 Unknown. (2010). Trans-Antarctica Expedition 1914-17. Available: http://www.coolantarctica.com/Antarctica%20fact %20file/History/Ernest%20Shackleton_Trans-Antarctic_expedition4.htm. Last accessed 22nd July 2013.
31 Oxfam. (2013). Oxfam Purpose and Beliefs. Available: http://www.oxfam.org/en/about/what/purpose-and-beliefs. Last accessed 22nd July 2013.
32 Jim Collins & Jerry I. Porras (2005). Built to Last: Successful Habits of Visionary Companies. London: Random House. p52.
33 Jim Collins & Jerry I. Porras (2005). Built to Last: Successful Habits of Visionary Companies. London: Random House. p52.
34 Jim Collins (2001). Good to Great. London: Random House. p42.
35 Keith Yamashita & Sandra Spataro (2004). Unstuck. New York: Portfolio. p85.
36 Jack Welch & Suzy Welch (2005). Winning. London: Harper Collins. p181.
37 John Maxwell (1998). The 21 Irrefutable Laws of Leadership. Nashville, TN: Thomas Nelson. p178.
38 Daniel H Pink (2011). Drive: The Surprising Truth About What Motivates Us. Edinburgh: Canongate Books.
39 Stephen R Covey (2004). The 8th Habit: From Effectiveness to Greatness. London: Simon & Schuster. p5.
40 Jim Collins & Jerry I. Porras (2005). Built to Last: Successful Habits of Visionary Companies. London: Random House. p35.
41 Ross Toro. (2011). Slacker Staffers: Disengaged in the Workplace (Infographic). Available: http://www.livescience.com/16881-engaged-employees-job-satisfaction-infographic.html. Last accessed 25th July 2013.
42 People Metrics. (2011). Calculating the Cost of Employee Disengagement. Available: http://www.peoplemetrics.com/blog/calculating-the-cost-of-employee-disengagement/. Last accessed 25th July 2013.
43 Valve (2012). HANDBOOK FOR NEW EMPLOYEES: A fearless adventure in knowing what to do when no one's there telling you what to do.. Washington: Valve. .
44 Valve (2012). HANDBOOK FOR NEW EMPLOYEES: A fearless adventure in knowing what to do when no one's there telling you what to do.. Washington: Valve. .
45 Oliver Chiang. (2011). Valve And Steam Worth Billions. Available:

http://www.forbes.com/sites/oliverchiang/2011/02/15/valve-and-steam-worth-billions/. Last accessed 25th July 2013.

46 Unknown. (2013). organizational culture quotes. Available: http://quotes.dictionary.com/search/organizational+culture?page=1. Last accessed 29th July 2013.

47 Unknown. (2013). The Importance Of Organisational Culture Change. Available: http://www.cultureconsultancy.com/links/the-importance-of-organisational-culture-change/#. Last accessed 30th July 2013.

48 Jack Welch & Suzy Welch (2005). Winning. London: Harper Collins. p84.

49 Unknown. (2013). Famous Quotes on Culture. Available: http://www.culturedyn.com/Famous%20Quotes%20on %20Culture.htm. Last accessed 30th July 2013.

50 Richard Branson (2008). Business Stripped Bare: Adventures of a global entrepreneur. London: Random House. p30.

51 John Maxwell (1998). The 21 Irrefutable Laws of Leadership. Nashville, TN: Thomas Nelson. p20.

52 John Maxwell (1998). The 21 Irrefutable Laws of Leadership. Nashville, TN: Thomas Nelson. p37.

53 John Maxwell (2007). The 21 Indispensable Qualities of a Leader : Becoming the Person Others Will Want to Follow. Nashville: Thomas Nelson.

54 John Maxwell (1998). The 21 Irrefutable Laws of Leadership. Nashville, TN: Thomas Nelson. p20.

55 John Maxwell (1998). The 21 Irrefutable Laws of Leadership. Nashville, TN: Thomas Nelson. p45.

56 Jim Collins (2001). Good to Great. London: Random House. p21.

57 John Maxwell (1998). The 21 Irrefutable Laws of Leadership. Nashville, TN: Thomas Nelson. p126.

58 Jim Collins & Jerry I. Porras (2005). Built to Last: Successful Habits of Visionary Companies. London: Random House. p212.

59 Jim Collins & Jerry I. Porras (2005). Built to Last: Successful Habits of Visionary Companies. London: Random House. p117.

60 Jack Welch & Suzy Welch (2005). Winning. London: Harper Collins. p17.

61 Jim Collins (2001). Good to Great. London: Random House. p50.

62 Jim Collins & Jerry I. Porras (2005). Built to Last: Successful Habits of Visionary Companies. London: Random House. p88.

63 Ben Drury. (2013). Praise and Punishment = Culture!. Available: http://www.cogiva.com/2013/06/11/praise-and-punishment-culture/. Last accessed 22nd July 2013.

64 Paddi Lund (1997). Building a Happiness-Centred Business. 2nd ed. Queensland, Australia: Solutions Press. p10.

65 Jack Welch & Suzy Welch (2005). Winning. London: Harper Collins. p98.

66 Jack Welch & Suzy Welch (2005). Winning. London: Harper Collins. p167.

67 Unknown. (2013). Nordstrom. Available: http://en.wikipedia.org/wiki/Nordstrom. Last accessed 27th August 2013.

68 Stephen R Covey (2004). The 8th Habit: From Effectiveness to Greatness. London: Simon & Schuster. p15.

69 Theodore Roosevelt Malloch (2008). Virtuous Business. Nashville: Thomas Nelson. p61.

70 Jack Welch & Suzy Welch (2005). Winning. London: Harper Collins. p56.

71 Jim Collins & Jerry I. Porras (2005). Built to Last: Successful Habits of Visionary Companies. London: Random House. p138.

72 Richard Branson (2008). Business Stripped Bare: Adventures of a global entrepreneur. London: Random House. p37.

73 Jim Collins (2001). Good to Great. London: Random House. p121.

74 Unknown. (2013). Office Space. Available: http://en.wikiquote.org/wiki/Office_Space. Last accessed 30th August 2013.

75 Josh Dunlop. (2012). Top 20 Most Awesome Company Offices. Available: http://www.incomediary.com/top-20-most-awesome-company-offices. Last accessed 30th August 2013

76 William J. Billy. (2012). The Art of Designing a Modern Office. Available: http://www.luckett-farley.com/the-art-of-designing-a-modern-office/. Last accessed 2nd September 2013.

77 The Juggle. (2011). Why Office Design Matters. Available: http://blogs.wsj.com/juggle/2011/08/04/why-office-design-matters/. Last accessed 2nd September 2013.

78 Tim Smedley. (2012). Workplace design: how office space is becoming fun again. Available: http://www.theguardian.com/money/2012/feb/17/workplace-design-office-space-fun. Last accessed 2nd September 2013.

79 Tim Smedley. (2012). Workplace design: how office space is becoming fun again. Available: http://www.theguardian.com/money/2012/feb/17/workplace-design-office-space-fun. Last accessed 2nd September 2013.

80 Inc Magazine. (2013). 10 Office Design Tips to Foster Creativity. Available: http://www.inc.com/ss/jessica-stillman/10-office-design-tips-foster-creativity. Last accessed 2nd September 2013.

81 Jack Welch & Suzy Welch (2005). Winning. London: Harper Collins. p15.

82 Theodore Roosevelt Malloch (2008). Virtuous Business. Nashville: Thomas Nelson. PXX

83 Theodore Roosevelt Malloch (2008). Virtuous Business. Nashville: Thomas Nelson. p87.

Made in the USA
Charleston, SC
15 September 2013